better together*

*This book is best read together, grownup and kid.

 akidsco.com

a
kids
book
about

a kids book about

BANKING

by Mehrsa Baradaran

a
kids
book
about

Printed in the United States of America.

A Kids Book About books are available online: *akidsco.com*

To share your stories, ask questions, or inquire about bulk
purchases (schools, libraries, and nonprofits), please use
the following email address: *hello@akidsco.com*

Print book ISBN: 978-1-958825-17-4
Ebook ISBN: 978-1-958825-18-1

Designed by Rick DeLucco
Edited by Jennifer Goldstein and Emma Wolf

The author would like to thank Asia Meana.

To Cyra, Lucia, and Ramona,
my moonlight, starlight, and butterfly.

Intro

My curiosity about (or, maybe more accurately, obsession with) financial policy started during the 2008 financial crisis. As a Wall Street banking lawyer, I had a front row seat as real life events debunked every single thing I had learned about money, banking, and economics.

The crisis pulled the curtain on an opaque and complex financial system that no one, especially the people in charge, fully understood. Yet their risky decisions rippled across the entire globe, causing real hardship. Banks control the flow and distribution of money and credit, which gives them the power to make or break our dreams.

I have spent the last decade writing about reforms toward a fairer credit system. Now, I am working to envision a financial system that rains down opportunity ladders and lucky breaks to as many kids as possible.

The original meaning of the word credit (credere) is "to believe." When my family applied for permission to come to America, this country gave us credit—they believed us and believed in us. I believe that every child has a unique genius of their own. My secret hope is that a kid reading this book becomes a magic money genie!

WHAT IS

A BANK?

Banks are where our money goes.

Banks are where the money grows.

Banks are the engines
that make the money go.

They look like regular businesses,
but they act like a magic trick.

Why do we trust the
bank with our money?

Because there are strict laws about
what banks can do with our money.

What do banks do with our money?

 MAGIC!

Specifically, they lend it.

They plant it like a seed
that grows into a money tree.
(Insert brain bookmark here.)

But before you can see money magic, you have to erase some things from your brain.

Do you see any banks with vaults full of gold bars and diamonds in there?

Erase. Delete.

Now, pull up all your mental pictures of money. Do you see coins and dollars?

Wipe those pictures clean!

So, what do
MONEY AND BANKING
look like?

Nothing, and everything.
It's all just digits on a screen!

The bank keeps track of money on a digital cloud, knowing exactly which numbers on a screen are **YOUR** money and which numbers are **MY** money.

Let's take a trip to demonstrate:

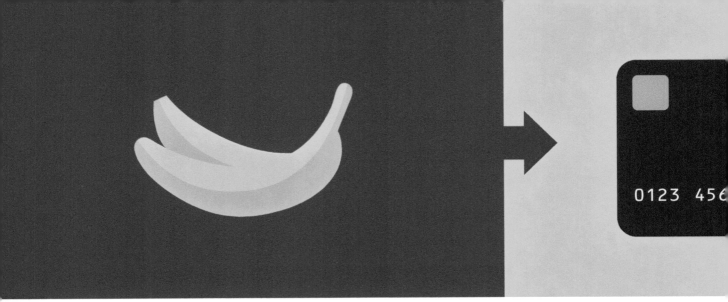

Imagine you're checking out at the grocery store, buying 5 bananas for $5.

(Sheesh, when did bananas get so expensive?)

Now, ask a grownup for their plastic money card.

OK, swipe it or insert it.
Hold it there.
Don't remove it!

I said do not—

REMOVE YOUR CARD!
RIGHT NOW
RIGHT NOW
RIGHT NOW
BEEP BEEEEEP!

Phew. You did it!

Now walk out with the bananas.

DID YOU SEE IT?

While we were following orders from the aggressive beep-beep box, the cloud did the math and sent the money from your grownup's account to the grocery store.

The grocery store's bank and your bank are 2 nodes on a super secure banking wire, channel, or current.

A current is where *current*-cy (get it?) can flow from you to the store so you can walk out with 5 bananas.

The banks were talking through the rude beep-beep box. It's like a walkie talkie—let's call it a money talkie—that the banks use, in the cloud, to beam money to each other.

AND THAT, MY FRIEND, IS WHAT BANKING IS.

Banks aren't buildings full of gold

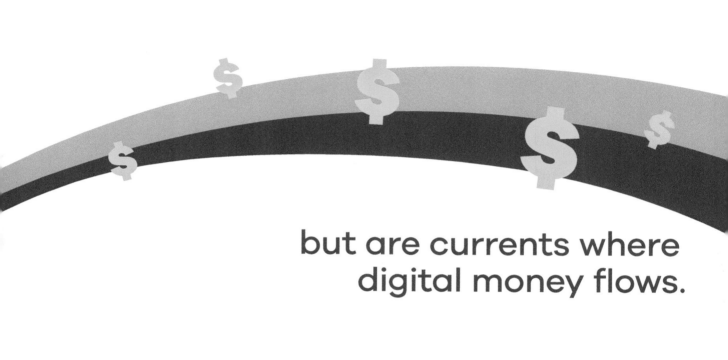

but are currents where
digital money flows.

Banks help the money flow.

And they also make
the money grow.

It's true!

Because money is magic—
make-money-out-of-nothing magic.

Which, to me, is the best kind!

Every time a bank gives someone a loan to buy something like a house or car, they are creating money that wasn't there before (loans plant seeds that grow into money trees).

How?

By letting other people borrow it.

A bank loan is a contract:
the bank gives you a big chunk of
money for your dream house and
you promise to pay them back.

When you pay back a loan, you don't
just return the money you borrowed.
You pay a little extra each month.

That's called interest.

What makes interest so *interest*ing
is that it's the cost of money.

That's right,
MONEY COSTS MONEY!

Interest is how money grows and it grows fast, so you have to watch it carefully if you're on the paying side of interest.

Nothing in the world grows
more than money does.

Because...

MONEY I

S MAGIC!

Even the serious and seriously boring college books call banks "magic money multipliers."

There's just 1 catch:

The magic money multiplier only works if people believe it works.

(Remember that brain bookmark?)

Everyone with money in the bank has a record that shows how much they have at the bank (even though the money isn't really there).

And usually, this works fine, because most people don't need all their money at one time. So they trust the bank and forget about it.

Then banks can continue their money-growing magic.

But things happen, and people get scared that the bank will lose their money.

They lose trust in the banks.

And without trust, the whole thing stops.

First 1 person gets scared,
then more people get scared,
and then everyone gets scared
(that's called a **BANK PANIC**).

And when people are panicked, they
run to the bank to get their money
(that's called a **BANK RUN**).

After a major bank run that turned
into the Great Depression, President
Roosevelt said, "the only thing we
have to fear is fear itself."

But the money isn't there. It's out there planting seeds to grow into money trees, and you can't just yank the seeds back because someone already used them to buy a house!

So the money multiplier stops and the engines freeze. When this happens, it's really hard on people.

The magic only works if people keep believing in it.

That's right—I said you have to believe in money for it to work.

As long as everyone keeps their money in the bank and trusts the system, the money will continue to move and grow.

Think about it: we use the $ and number symbols (for example, $1.23) to buy bananas or boats because we all believe in those numbers.

ISN'T THAT WILD?!
MONEY IS MAGIC!

Money is the language we all speak.

My kids spoke money way before they could read.

I bet you did too.

 MONEY IS A CURRENT—A WAVE OF POTENTIAL, HOPE, AND ENERGY.

 MONEY IS AN IDEA WE ALL AGREE ON.

 MONEY IS VALUABLE BECAUSE WE ALL BELIEVE IT HAS VALUE.

 MONEY IS A PIXEL ON A SCREEN.

 AND, HISTORICALLY SPEAKING, MONEY IS A VIRAL MEME.

And here's the last mind-blowing magic trick that money has up its sleeve: Money is the 1 thing on Earth we can never run out of.*

*Cue brain explosion!

By living and shopping and eating at restaurants, we make money valuable.

And our government prints as much as we need to use.

THAT'S RIGHT.

The only limit on money
is our bad ideas about money.

And I'm just going to be
real with you here:

There are lots of bad ideas
about money out there.

Bad money ideas are the reason
some people don't have enough to
eat or have to work all day and
all night just to have a house.

Even though money is an idea and abstraction, not having money is a real and hard reality.

THE GOOD NEWS IS THAT IDEAS CAN BE CHANGED.

Delete the bad ideas
and restart the engine.

Try to dream of the world
you would build if you had
all the money in the world.

Because we do.

And we can!

The only thing we need is hope
itself and trust in each other.

TRUST IS
THE VALUE OF MONEY.

TRUST FUELS
THE MAGIC MONEY MULTIPLIER.

TRUST IS
THE CURRENCY OF LOVE.

TRUST LIVES
IN OUR COMMUNITIES.

What if we trust in each other
enough to let our money
flow and grow?

Hope, trust, and dreams are renewable resources—the more we have, the more we make.

AND MONEY I

THAT NEV

S THE MAGIC
ER FAILS.

Outro

Transaction complete. Now you know about the banks. Our kids are already participating in the economy, whether they're aware of it or not. When they discover the ins and outs of money and banking, kids develop the tools to thrive, and to shape the world into a place they'll want to inhabit when they grow up.

Banking consists of rules that determine the way we play the game of life. My hope is that our kids will be inspired to learn these rules so that they can then tweak them to make the game more fair—and more fun—for everyone. We need our genius magic-money-multiplying magicians well-fed with good questions. Here are some, for starters:

1. Name someone or something you trust with all your heart. Why do you feel that way?

2. What is something you are curious about that no one you know really seems to understand? Maybe that's your unique and special genius!

3. When you think about your future, what are you most hopeful about? Say why.

The truth is that banking is more of a mystery than a science. And money is just plain practical magic. And that's how we can talk about these topics with kids, as well as Secretaries of the Treasury and banking regulators.

From The Author

I was born in Iran smack dab in the middle of a revolution that would transform my country into a war zone. By the time I could walk, Tehran was run by men with guns, my mother was in a political prison, and we were sleeping in our basement with gas masks at night listening to Iraqi bombs fall around us. I saw injustice all around me. I never got used to the taste of fear.

My lucky streak began when I was 8 and my family was granted political asylum and allowed to live in America. My mom got a job at a dry cleaners, my dad studied for tests, and we got a Chevy Chevette. We drove from book mobiles to libraries, from schools in California to schools in New York City, so I could freely read and live freely.

Having lived in poverty and privilege, I know how profoundly our environment shapes our lives. I'm glad my daughters won't know hardship but I can't call it justice. That is why I write the books I write.

 @mehrsabaradaran   Mehrsa Baradaran

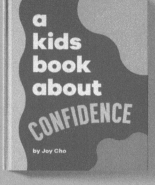

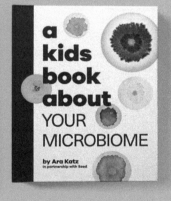

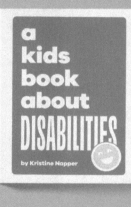

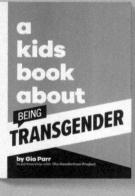